WHERE THE SKY IS A WALL

Poops

Poems

by

ANGELA HOOPER

First Edition August 2023

Cover Photograph by Angela Hooper

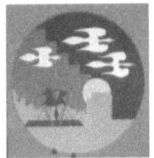

Village Books Press
Oklahoma City, OK

This book is for my entire family.

Forgiveness is the greatest gift
we can give to each other.

TABLE OF CONTENTS

My Name is Angela

Which means Angel
as though addition of wings
makes my posture straighter.
In reality

I am a larvae
pulsating half-moon
concealed in moist darkness
taking in liquid.
I constantly

test the sides
of this sac that holds me,
checking for remnants of a spine
to crawl to freedom.
It is the choice

only an Angel would make,
willing to be born again
after having found
the wings did not fit.
The Angels on earth

have all sinned
enough to acquire compassion
which is what I hope for when I emerge,
or at least to be optimistic.

The Girl Seed

I see you poking up
from the ground
thin and brown
from all the sun
you have taken.
I see my own
leathered bark,
cracks that expose
my middle meat,
white and pithy
where the worms
still crawl to my toes
and feed on memory.

From the distance I can see
where you have lost symmetry
to the thunderous winds
of spring and summer.
Even when the night
is left with just the stars
to light the lawn,
I can still see you
in the back yard
between the hibiscus
and the mimosa,
an awkward
ugly old elm
battered, resilient
the one I could never love.

My Life as a Cabinet

For Billy Collins
In honor of his visit to Oklahoma City University, April 6, 2005

I am the lively wood brought in from the outside,
softened by droplets of grease and water
that have flown across this kitchen
for over 40 years.

I am a cavity of planks smelling of spices
with scattered boxes of cereal
forgotten packs of soy sauce,
left with only doors for tongues.

My fear has nailed me to this wall
where I have listened
to the echo of midnight voices
looking for answers amongst the clutter.

I wonder if I am normal having stayed
in the same spot for so long,
my woodgrain trapped in a moment
with all those dead cells collecting.

The paint is wet as it comes out of the can.
It holds the power of transformation,
sustenance the size of a drop,
toes that start to wiggle again.

The Redlands

For Dad

His parents kept the crop money
buried in a Folger's can
in the dirt floor of their garage.
His father had to dig it up
for the kids when his mother died.
In the spring her hydrangeas
bloomed in perfect indigo,
the soil fed by the nails
she dutifully planted.
They knew what it took
to cultivate the Redlands.

They watched
Billy Graham
on the television
in the front room
with its tiny screen
and three channels.
They listened
as he talked about
Paul's letters
and how we will all be
judged by our secret lives.

My father was a plow
ripping up the land
from the time he was seven,
sack lunch and cigarettes
in hand, until he too became
the dust floating past
his beloved baseball field.
A boy with a man's voice
and nowhere else to go.

I was a rake.
As a child I used to float my
foot over the red dirt like a
visitor.
I used to mark time
by watching the doorstep of
the tin shack
where you were born
sink further into the prairie.

You were the knotted holes
in the wooden outhouse they
used until
I was in high school.
They were the red net
Christmas stockings stuffed
with expensive fruit and rock
candies
given to grandchildren who
did not fully understand the
sacrifice of those gifts.

Until the tractors finished
scraping off the lot,
I had not remembered how
red the dirt was underneath
the heaving piles of concrete
and asphalt left from the
blast.
We take what comfort we
can in this flat and desolate
land not even Timothy
McVeigh could change.

We are the roots
four generations deep

planted in this red clay dirt
just close enough
to water
to survive.

Wetumka

The fields were my backyard,
miles and miles of barbed wire fence
held up by weathered posts
nailed tight against the wind.
The only shapes were
the clouds of dust
my tractor left behind.
I saw my path forward
in the tunnels
the prairie dogs made.

He was tall, built like an ox.
He wore the same overalls every day,
except on Sundays.
His whole life was about
worshipping a God I never knew
and plowing the fields.
He saw me as his farm hand.

I learned early to hate being
beaten by the wind,
the way his arm would swing
when he'd yank my overalls down,
whipping me in the barn
as I counted the fish heads outside
drying on the fence posts,
because I knew
when he was finished
we'd go fishing.

My Mother's Voice

I remember her voice in my head
that afternoon when she told me
now was the time to act.
The woman my father craved
had turned my mother's house
into a darkened cave.

From her grave she sent me out
to confront my father,
and reclaim what belonged to us,
to pick up as many pieces
as I possibly could,
and briefly pretend
he wasn't the one
who broke us.

He remained focused
on his wet cave dreams
until I shifted the center
away from that woman
and back to me,
the one who found
my own power
because I heard
my dead mother's voice.

Thief

He never let us forget
he saw us as pennies
with monuments of stone
on our back sides,
mortared and planted
shinning in his path
as he dangled the promise
we would be
rewarded.

She started with coffee,
months before my mother's death,
her words a salve for his loses,
so he gobbled and gave,
let her posse into his house,
turned my mother's bedroom
into her personal drug den.
Everything saved in a lifetime
siphoned.

He never apologized
even after the police came
for his final interview
one week exactly
before his own death.
Tarnished and ashamed
he threw the final dagger,
confessed his complicity
knowing she would be
exonerated.

Daddy

For my daughter, Alesia
August 24th, 2017

It's raining hard here today
making puddles in the asphalt
in the middle of our prairie,
the one that will not
be denied.

They sent your brothers
off to fight the war,
leaving you to fight your own
with a tractor in the fields,
smoking cigarettes by the barn.
Was that what turned
your heart black?

I have always been scared of you,
stuck in the barbed wire snare,
of a man who only knew himself,
trapped in the Walmart sentiment
of black and white,
oblivious to the gray
of his own children.

You put your foot to the metal
and turned us over
like rotted roots.
It was so much easier
to put your boot
into our faces,
than to ever admit
you were wrong.

Yesterday morning
I saw my daughter
in her cheer uniform
and I cried tears of joy.
You know what it means, Daddy.
The girl who looks like me, who
looks like you,
has finally given me back
my pretty red heart
you bit in two!

Five years, if you want to know,
trying to take back
all the love
you squandered
like flood waters
coming too fast
to be absorbed
by the drought
of the life you lived.

I'm leaving you here
in your fields
as I drive away
from your little pink house
one last time
with the dust flying, Daddy.
I am the emancipated
ghost you always
looked through,
and I am done
with you!

Scar Tissue

The fibers have grown
in place of the scab,
an outward sign
that I am healing.

My fingers have grown
used to the texture
of these new tissues,
markers of memory.

The scars have whitened
with time, so much they
can only be truly seen
inside the lining of my gut.

All I need is water,
carbohydrates and fibroblasts
to give me the collagen
I need to mute you.

In the end I am the winner.
I merely lost perfect skin
and gained beautiful survival,
while your story fades.

Heir Apparent

For my mother, Sue Ann Clemons Smith, and my grandfather, Edgar Captain Clemons

By looking at my white face you cannot see the Creek ancestry that my mother gave me. A stranger must see her olive skin and brown eyes to begin to understand. Her father, my grandfather, was one quarter Creek Indian. His mother, my great grandmother, was what they spurned as a half-breed because they thought they were righteous enough to judge her for what they perceived to be my great-great-grandmother's sin, who could have easily been raped by a white man, or worse, simply fell in love because in his arms she was able to forget the genocide waged on her people.

We will never know their true stories. We only have the stories your father told about the government camps erected on the site where the capitol grounds now stand, tenements without heat or running water, and your father with his sling-shot hunting squirrels for food. I don't believe that the Creeks were heathens any more than you did. They have a language that still survives, the Green Corn Dance is still performed, and a belief in the Master-of-Breath, a God he could never find, because by then the government had already taken the terrapin shells and replaced them with poverty.

During his own life, he always claimed to be Cherokee because it made him feel more dignified, this man who collected books that filled up rooms; hundreds of biographies, works by Carl Sandburg, Mark Twain, Upton Sinclair, volumes about the wars, and a rare picture book I remember as a child that documented the great fire that ended the traveling tent shows of what became the Ringling Bros. and Barnum & Bailey Circus. He was always ashamed of his middle name, "Captain," because his mother did not realize it was a title to be earned and not a name to be given.

You with your big dark eyes and olive skin are still eating those squirrels. Sometimes when I catch your tears repelled by the fur on your tongue, I find myself reaching to pluck the fine strands from my own teeth. And I kiss them. Perhaps our story begins with the picture on my mantle of a young man beaming into the face of his infant daughter, you who are an eighth descended from a woman who was whole to me a mere sixteenth. No matter how we split this fraction, the laws of love and physics promise that there will always be another piece to split into infinity.

On the Road from Wetumka

The afternoon light
pierced their windshield
with prisms that absorbed
into their dashboard.
No radio ever played
because she could not be
calmed in the car.
Floating trash collected
in the floorboard
a torn and grimy map
of their shared topography.
When it started to rain
he refused to slow down
for her to go to the toilet,
so she rolled her window down
and fed her wet panties to the wipers.
She never even noticed
her three small children
strapped in the back seat,
their eyes perfect ellipses.

Hamloaf

The meat was always ground

Slightly pink from the mixture

Of blood and fat, a perfect texture

That if placed end to end without pause

Would have exhausted us all.

But the loaf was reprieve from broken glass,

Booming voice blasting at a moment's notice

Blissfully silenced by savory sweet gooey topping.

Passed from Grandpa, to my mother and to me.

Gone is the butcher shop

Where Grandpa bought the mix,

For Sunday meals and holidays.

I only have the yellowed piece of paper

Scrawled in Mother's tight little letters,

As if being committed to print

Would assure it would always

Be the same.

We Live and Die by Angels

We live and die by angels
the movement of their breath
the way they exhale without lungs
oblivious of how they cut the air
between you and them
undeterred
by physics.

Your memory is like a particle
that has caught a ray
illuminating everything
presumed lost
flooding the room
with just enough light
to not consume
but reflect.

I see them clearly
all the filters
you held up for him,
so he could knock
you down
instead of us.

I wonder if he
can see through
the dark ashes
of his lonely box
how you would
be the one
making the wings
now.

Forgiveness

For my mother, Sue Ann Clemons Smith

He was like the rapid oxidation of material
in the process of combustion, the release
of light and heat, energy expended
for the sole purpose of consumption.

The flame was only the visible part.
We lost our fingers and toes to his fire,
both of us forced to support our weight
on disfigured limbs that snap and fray with pressure.

I learned to see it as the skulls of Pol Phot
stacked in neat pyramids
to be worshiped and feared,
a million lips sealed shut!

This morning on my walk I saw
a garden path lined with stones
smooth and hard secured by the ground
that still holds treasures the fire could not destroy.

And I realized that some things
can actually be mourned.

The Darkness

For my brother, Steve

"This place right here, this skull between my ears, that is a bad neighborhood, and I should not be in there alone." Chester B, interview with JoJo Wright via Loudwire, February 17, 2017.

Your nights were filled by silent invitations to slip for a swim into the pools of ink that were your thoughts. As you dipped your limbs into the well, you willed away your own resonance, silenced the choir of his echoing voice, and swam like hell into that space where there was only you.

At first the darkness was a blanket warmed by the absorption of light from stars you thought you had trapped, until time turned you into just another passenger stranded in space trying to scale the walls of Black. Even on those precious days when you were shining, you were still invisible.

Your body was his kindling. He thought he had every right to use you for his own gratification. It all came down to consumption, the need to displace the weight of his crime with fluidity. You voluntarily extinguished your own light because Black was the only place you found comfort.

There are no expectations of air. It is just air, or so we thought. We had no idea that you were on an exploration to discover a new planet where you could finally breathe.

Doctor's Orders

For the intern who signed the
order to take my brother off life
support.

My name is not important.
I have a tag for that on my chest.
My white coat is my identity.
I do not need to be announced.
I am here because
I always wanted to be.

They keep coming
so many wizened lungs,
hearts grown too thick to beat
and their families
desperate for hope
I cannot give.

I hate Saturdays.
They follow Friday nights
when emergency surgeries
run into early morning
to clear the board
for the weekend.
I try to stick to my present
where I can attempt
to control the outcomes.
The families do not accept death.

I expect death
though I will always fight,
except that Saturday night
after I spent the day
saving her brother's life.
She gave it up,
signed the papers.

I complied with my signature,
then she hunted me down
to give me a hug.
I broke the rules,
I hugged her back.

An Innocent Question

It happened again today.
You got caught in my throat
on a Sunday afternoon
as the party was ending.
It felt like a lodged marble
preventing the air from passing
over my tongue into my lungs
as if the lining had somehow
become glued.

I struggled for words
your story held hostage
in my chest,
a perfect ball
in fetal position,
a human being,
an undefined life
punctuated by
premature death.

The question was innocent
meant to be loving,
but the final struggle
was just too much
for the narrow passages
of my chest to contain.
So I walked away
to the coke machine
put in a coin
and started over
hoping that I could
finish the story
this time.

What I've learned about your death so far...

That death remains unannounced
leaving me the one who will remember
the date, the day of the week,
what time it was,
when you took your last breath.

That everything is stuck in my chest
like a thousand pebbles lodged,
forcing me to breathe in half breaths,
my blood thick and pooled,
a wound that resists care and light.

That I find myself at the store
in front of the rows of merchandise,
wondering why my body will only release
one pebble at a time and if it will
still hurt this much next time.

That we get so damn busy conspiring
against doing the right thing
we do everything else instead.
I was so afraid of being the one burned,
I missed the fire that consumed you.

That reflecting on the last kiss
I planted on your clammy forehead
may be the only thing that will help me
teach my body to process
the shards of glass gathered in my gut
to fine smooth bits
that I hope eventually pass.

The Apartment

I was asked.
I told them everything
the surgery, the stroke,
twelve hours of begging
to pull the plug
and being too numb
to actually cry.

I didn't tell them
about your lost life.
No walkable paths
in your living room,
how it took four people
bagging up trash
for two days straight
before we even saw
the remaining
surfaces of you.

My husband asked
for your television.
We gave your tools
to your friend.
We cleaned and cleaned
and painted everything.
On the day we signed
the papers,
we drove away
thankful that door
was finally closed.

Sunset

In our father's prime
he started every morning
with a full pot of coffee
and a half pack
of cigarettes.
He believed
the swirls
would save him.
This is how our father
handled dread.

The biggest lesson
our father taught us
was how to have
our boundaries crashed.
He only saw
his own reflection
in the water.
This is how he taught us
to accept being silenced
like fish.

As the last rays of light
filter through the trees
casting shadows
on the lawn like a map,
do we have the courage
to see our ability
to challenge the pull
created by the shadow
of the trunk and limbs?
Can we see the filtering light
as we each try to teach ourselves
how to become
one of his survivors?

The Survivor Tree

For my sister, Alesia

There are no vacation albums
just the tapes we played
for each other
on drunken Friday nights.
How could we have predicated
the blast that would
split our trunks
sending husbands and dreams
floating away like paper?

The history of our violence
has already left us
cautious and cheated.
It has taken time
to perfect the digestion
of all the loosened bark
that has gathered
under our nails
as we have climbed back.

We cannot stop
the coming of winter.
We are deciduous beings.
Our winterized dreams
will still emerge.
Even bombs cannot destroy seeds
with the smallest of hairs
that take in the water first.

Easter 2017

As I back out against the traffic
I try not to mourn
the beautiful language
we once shared,
my shell fingered and pricked,
shattered by awkward pauses.

As I drive home
I think about the journey,
what it's like to realize
the one I always loved
has become the one
who has left me fractured.

I am a reluctant Christian.
I feel every pebble of this road
with my pink and tender feet.
I resent the changes in the asphalt,
the whiteness of the concrete,
now stained with yellow of me.

I drive home without the radio.
I want to remember
the sound of your violin
before he stole everything
that made those bright strings ring,
before his death
reconfigured us.

Silence

Everyone has their reasons
for picking their own corners
to cling to silence
in the hope we are not
forced to speak first.

To articulate means
making another circle
that grows more treacherous
as grooves wear deeper
into the floor we share.

There is no tolerance
for broken glass recollections
that splits our shared light
into so many prisms
we cannot find ourselves.

We want compensation
for the lives we came from.
We just didn't realize
that we come
so poorly equipped
to collect.

Recovery

The hardest part
is letting go
of a garden
tilled and seeded,
populated by
well-fed worms,
oxygenating,
breathing,
alive.

I have to let go
of the heart breaking
truth about us
and your estimation
that I have fallen
short.

Your angry heart
shows no sign of retreat.
I am no longer yours.
It's just me now
claiming my scars,
cycling.

I am a dried up field
with all my vegetation
lying down flat
along my curvature,
starved of light
waiting it out,
hoping.

Wistful

It used to be passion.

It could have been hope.

Now it is a hollow drum

That beats in a rhythm

I am loath to learn.

I gave it my all

But you were stronger.

I am a mortal sling shot

Tethered in that continuum

Between love and hate,

A resignation waiting to be tendered.

Raven
Our Black Angel

The blooms of the redbuds
are small and tight
this year.

There has not been enough
rain to penetrate
root systems.

Blossoms have come to remind
us that there is
still life.

We want the turgid displays
of more spectacular
days past.

We are greedy to count
the dead like blossoms
falling down.

Foolish girls, we see her
as gone but she has
only changed.

Breaking the Silence

For the one out of three women
who were molested as children

The first cut was not really a cut
but more of a thump
as he waited until our mother
laid me down on the bed unattended
to rinse out a diaper.
Me only a few days old
as he jumped on the mattress
laughing with glee
and dumped me screaming
head first onto the floor.

The second cut was not really a cut either
but more an opportunity.
The trunk was left open or maybe
he stole the keys from her purse.
When he has done fingering my parts
he closed the lid in hopes
that I would not live to tell.
I remember his laugh as she unlocked it,
that terrifying chuckle.

I was twelve when he
pulled me into his room.
I fought in silent terror
as my clothes were stripped,
writhing as he touched
before he stroked his own
and tried to give me the deepest cut.
I managed to get away
grabbed my clothes from the floor
stumbled back into the bathroom

where I got dressed and cried.
My first time being naked.
Not realizing just how long it
was going to take
to heal that one.

The Ape

Fear and anger
were the only things
shining in your eyes.
You moved our arms
as if we were puppets
stealing my ability
to form circles of light.

With a marginal shift
of your superior weight
my hips were pinned.
I had to learn
to read in braille
to survive a sighted world
blind to us.

This is where I
have stood silent
for decades
with your weight
upon my back
always ready
to swing me like a tree.

Washing it Away

The hymen does not need
to be broken for there
to have been a breach.
The poisonous suds
still wash around the drain
down into the pipes,
where they are taken back
into a river or lake
or a treatment plant
where the chemicals
conspire to produce
a new substance
they will sell
as bottled water.

The Ledge

Is it a rose rock cliff
like one of the quasi mountains
at Roman Nose Park where the eye
gets distracted by beauty
and forgets it is a treacherous
place for a foot?

Is it a slab of concrete
poured generations ago by men
paid by the hour, in hopes
that it will withstand water
enough to keep all those
grains of sand trapped?

Is it veneered by brick
or perhaps luxuriant marble
impervious to penetration
yet renders a perfect echo
of child's inaudible voice
recounting the unspeakable?

Will I find out after all these years
that it is really just particle board
or glass or even lowly paper?
It is no matter.
It is still a ledge.
And I am still stuck.

Destruction

On the Demolition of the Terrace Executive Building
2809 NW Expressway, Oklahoma City, September 19, 2008

I am broken like that—
walls imploded, scars
whitened with time
so much so that they
can only be truly seen
inside the lining of my gut.

My concrete in random piles
fallen into nebulous monuments
to the places I have been,
each one a poem
on a napkin or a page ripped
from a journal,
all of it lost now
to the piles.

I am broken like that—
a mouth full of steel tongues
trying to get my story out,
with too many languages
filling up my throat at once
so that all of my tongues
fall flat like cut wires
with nothing left to say.

There is no center.
The right half is gone,
destroyed by the wrecking ball
leaving me
without light
without color
without direction.

The Movie Poem

The movie of my life
rolls across
my bathroom mirror,
the images lined up
like the eighteen years
of school pictures
I dragged to my therapist
every week
looking for peace
in chronological order.
Sometimes it was dangerous.

My mind begins to think
the damnedest things
like how my father
always preferred silence,
how my mother
hated him out loud,
and how my reflection
flattens out
to thin wavering lines
from the memories.

Today I see my own
reflection looking back
in perfect focus
with less than perfect hair
in a sale rack dress,
my ragged nails
carefully tucked,
with a fresh
understanding
not everything
has a happy ending.

How to Stand Like a Tree

Do not regret that we are not
hibiscus, tall and slender
standing against the fence
red, white, and purple.
Do not regret that we are not
chosen to be the Mimosa
with pink spikes of musk,
that bloom for a short season.

We are the Elms
the ones that thrive
even in awkward places
where we spent
our adolescence
casting our seeds
without reverence.
Even though our crowns
are brown, now
thinned to ribbons,
we still reach up.

Fear not the appetite
that sends you back
to the middle of your trunk
where neither the bite of insects
nor the burrowing of worms
penetrate the thickened fiber
developed from our refusal
to surrender.

Learning to Paint

I gave up poetry for painting.
I like the way
air bubbles stay trapped
below the surface
and form little patterns
just before gravity
flattens them out,
the way one color spreads
into slightly different shades
and then becomes one again
when the paint dries.
There are no blank pages here.

With a roller in my hand
I am not afraid of metaphor.
Two shelves of opened paint cans,
a half-painted hallway,
a spare bedroom
that screams for more color.
It all rhymes perfectly.

I gave up poetry
for painting,
so I could teach myself
how to move a trowel
through mud
across the ceiling,
standing on a broken stool
late at night in my kitchen
and find the face of angels
staring back at me.

Where the Sky is a Wall

For my mother

It was the kind of day
where the sky is a wall,
filled with clouds of puffy balls,
some of them the consistency
of burlap with frayed edges,
breaking down softly
across the horizon into wisps
of the finest strands,
that invite the eye
to continue.

Where the sky is a wall,
I only have to think of you
a sky filled with puffy balls
with frayed edges
softly breaking down
to the finest strands,
the distance between the wisps
open arms of abundance,
the kind of days
that invite the heart
to continue.

It was that kind of day
that I decided the wall of the sky
would not defeat me,
that all my ridged edges
had softened into your wisps,
breaths taken in memory
of you who held fast
to the fine stands,
a final vow of love,
an invitation to my own will
to continue.

Night Stalkers

We were born night stalkers
taught from the beginning
to make peace with darkness,
told to choke hard
on the "O" in hope.

It was a gift or so they thought
to teach us about the sky
fixed on that one piece of night
where we could find
the part that makes us,
part of this stone.

All we know is that indelible place
where our hearts darken,
the one that makes us seek
the ultimate explanation
of a life lived
the way we did.

Even in the face of physical assault,
I still tried to find courage to nurture,
invoke the power of belief,
called myself "mother,"
learned to own my failures.

Like tonight where I am
a new midnight blue stone,
camouflaged by the very night
that has asked me to be honest
as to whether or not…

I actually fear death.

On Claiming My Space

For my daughter, Alesia

I am standing here
at the bottom
ready to climb.
I never thought I had
the courage to take
this hill of jagged rocks
that mock my ability
to believe.

I thought I had to stay silent
as the soil under my feet
turned brick hard
from walking around
without direction.
The trail has become
circuitous as a noose,
and I must change.

Every step will be
straight up.
I am wearing
sturdy boots,
and have brought
extra water
so that if I face
too much at once
it will keep my throat
from being parched,
unable to speak the words
that keep me
moving.

I am the descendant
of people from Kansas
who came to Oklahoma
in their loaded wagons
looking for land.
And I am the descendant
of First Americans
who were relocated
without provisions,
who also came
for the land.

I no longer have
a fear of falling.
I have already lived
amongst the others
who have fallen,
some of us more than once.
With every step
I feel my blood pulsating,
allowing my body
to release death.

There will not be a parade
when I make it to the top.
I will still stand alone
proudly looking
across the horizon
at the blooming Redbuds
dressed in magenta,
and I will ask God
to make me Pink
like that again.

ACKNOWLEDGEMENTS

Maria Veres, thank you for the initial editing of this manuscript. Your patience and expertise are invaluable.

Thank you, Ken Hada, for your encouragement, reading my manuscript, and providing a quote.

Bill Boudreau, I appreciate your technical support, setting my book cover text, and manuscript publishing guidance.

I thank Terri Cummings, Village Books Press, for helping me put this collection together and for being a friend.

Also, I thank all my poet friends, especially Spontaneous Bob, for all their support.

ABOUT THE AUTHOR

Angela Hooper has lived in Oklahoma City all of her life and has written poetry since she was 12. She received a BA in English from the University of Central Oklahoma.

Her affiliation with the Individual Artists of Oklahoma gave her many opportunities to both read her own work and host monthly readings. She co-hosts Oklahoma Voices' Full Circle Bookstore Poetry & Open Mic as well as Oklahoma Poetry House @ 1515 Lincoln Poetry & Open Mic in Oklahoma City. She has been published in *The Mom Egg*, *Crosstimbers,* and the Woody Guthrie anthology, *Ain't Gonna Be Treated This Way*. She lives with her husband of 20 years and their teenage daughter.

www.ingramcontent.com/pod-product-compliance
Lightning Source LLC
Chambersburg PA
CBHW031904170626
46807CB00004B/1883